The Ordination
of Women
to the Priesthood

REFERENCE
of Draft Legislation
to the Diocesan Synods
1990

Memorandum by the Standing Committee
and Background Papers

GS Misc 336

CHURCH HOUSE PUBLISHING
Church House, Great Smith Street, London SW1P 3NZ

ISBN 0 7151 3733 6

Published 1990 for the General Synod of the Church of England by
Church House Publishing

GS Misc 336

Printed in England by Tasprint Ltd., South Woodford, London E18 1HB

Contents

Prefatory Note

On the instructions of the Standing Committee of the General Synod, I am circulating herewith a Memorandum by the Committee which constitutes the Formal Reference to the Diocesan Synods of the Draft Priests (Ordination of Women) Measure and of the Draft Canons associated with it. Appended to the Memorandum and circulated herewith are four items:

These are:

(1) The text of the referred Measure and Canons;

(2) The text of the Ordination of Women (Financial Provisions) Measure;

(3) An explanatory note relating to the referred Measure and Canons and also to the Financial Provisions Measure;

(4) The draft of a Code of Practice, prepared by the House of Bishops for use in conjunction with the draft legislation.

The Standing Committee's Memorandum makes clear that the Diocesan Synods are required to respond to the Formal Reference by *30 November 1991*. Diocesan Synod Secretaries are asked to report using a prescribed form, which is being sent to them separately (under reference DC(90) 8).

April 1990

W D PATTINSON
Secretary-General

DRAFT PRIESTS (ORDINATION OF WOMEN) MEASURE
DRAFT CANON C 4B (OF WOMEN PRIESTS) AND
DRAFT AMENDING CANON NO 13
Reference Under Article 8
Memorandum by the Standing Committee

INTRODUCTION

1. The General Synod has had under consideration since July 1988 the draft *Priests (Ordination of Women) Measure* and two associated Canons: draft *Canon C 4B (Of Women Priests)* and draft *Amending Canon No 13*. Over the same period, the General Synod has also had under consideration a second draft Measure - the draft *Ordination of Women (Financial Provisions) Measure*. Both draft Measures, together with the draft Canons associated with the first of them, have now completed the Revision Stage on the floor of the Synod.

2. The draft *Priests (Ordination of Women) Measure* and the two draft *Canons* associated with it have been designated as business within Article 8 of the Constitution of the General Synod. Accordingly, before the General Synod can consider these items for Final Approval, they must be referred to the diocesan synods for approval. Only if a majority of the Diocesan Synods indicate their approval can the General Synod proceed in each case to the Final Approval Stage. Texts of the draft Measures and the associated Canons, as revised by the General Synod, accompany this Memorandum.

3. The draft *Ordination of Women (Financial Provisions) Measure* is not business within Article 8. The General Synod accordingly does *not* need the support of a majority of Diocesan Synods before considering the item for Final Approval. Nevertheless the General Synod judges that when Diocesan Synods have the draft *Priests (Ordination of Women) Measure* and the associated draft *Canons* before them, they ought also to be aware of the second *(Financial Provisions) Measure,* even though it is not within Article 8, and therefore is not the subject of a formal Reference. The *Financial Provisions Measure* is therefore being sent to you but it comes simply as a matter of background or supporting information.

4. There is a further item appended to this Memorandum but which (like the *Financial Provisions Measure)* is not part of the Formal Reference and therefore comes merely for information, namely the *Code of Practice* which the House of Bishops has prepared as an indication of the ways in which the Bishops will, if the draft legislation reaches the Statute Book, interpret it and apply it within their dioceses.

5.   When the General Synod was considering the draft Measure and the draft Canons, members had before them a document prepared by the House of Bishops, entitled *The Ordination of Women to the Priesthood: A Second Report by the House of Bishops* (GS 829). That Report, published by Church House Publishing (£4.50) is available from the Church House Bookshop. I am, however, sending you together with this Memorandum a digest of the Bishops' Report prepared on behalf of the House of Bishops by the Bishop of Crediton. Further copies of the Digest are available from the Church House Bookshop (Price £1.50;£62.50 (£1.25 each) for a pack of 50).

ACTION BY DIOCESAN SYNOD

6.   To comply with the requirements of Article 8, there needs to be from each diocesan synod a clear expression of approval or disapproval of the draft *Priests (Ordination of Women) Measure* and of the draft Canons associated with it. Each diocese is, therefore, asked to consider a motion in the following terms:

> 'That this Synod approves the proposals embodied in the draft *Priests (Ordination of Women) Measure* and in draft *Canon C 4B (Of Women Priests)* and draft *Amending Canon No. 13.'*

It will be appreciated that what the General Synod is seeking is a clear decision whether the diocesan synods approve the legislation in the form in which it now comes to them. What is sought is not a vague generalised assent to (nor disagreement with) the principle, but a specific indication of whether the Diocesan Synod supports (or does not support) the legislation in its present form.

7. As is customary on these occasions, the Standing Committee specifically asks that each diocesan synod should have before it a motion exactly in the terms set out in the previous paragraph and that it should be voted upon - for or against - in that form, *without amendment, and as a single motion*. This request is made to enable the General Synod to make an exact comparison between the voting in the different dioceses. Diocesan Synods are asked to vote by Houses.

8.   The number of those voting for and against the motion in each House and the number of declared abstentions, if any, should be recorded. Attention is invited to Rule 28(1)(h) of the Church Representation Rules which provides that if the votes of the Houses of Clergy and Laity are in favour of a matter referred under Article 8, then that matter shall be deemed to have been approved for the purposes of the said Article. Nevertheless, the Standing Committee asks that a vote should be taken on the matter in the House of Bishops of the diocesan synod, and that details of the voting in that House, and any abstentions, should be reported.

If exceptionally no vote is taken in the House of Bishops, this should be stated by the Secretary in his return (see para. 11 below). In connection with any voting in the House of Bishops, attention is also drawn to the Rule 28(1)(i) and (j). If in addition the Diocesan Bishop asks for his distinct opinion to be recorded separately, this too should be reported.

9. It may be that a diocesan synod, in the course of its consideration of the business now being referred, will wish to consider other motions, in addition to the motion officially prescribed in para. 6 above. Such motions may relate to the *Priests (Ordination of Women) Measure,* or to the draft *Canons* associated with it (all of which are referred under Article 8), or to the *Ordination of Women (Financial Provisions) Measure* or to the Bishops' Code of Practice. Where such additional motions are considered, the General Synod will wish to have the full text of all of them, and of any amendments that may be moved, whether or not the motion (or amendment) is carried. Rule 28(1)(h) applies only to the officially prescribed motion. *Accordingly, for any additional motion to be deemed to be carried, it must have the assent of the Synod in accordance with paragraph 28(1)(g),* unless the Diocesan Bishop or any ten members require that a separate vote of each House be taken.

CONSIDERATION BY DEANERY SYNODS

10. The Standing Committee asks diocesan synods to arrange to consult the deanery synods about this Reference. This is, of course, a matter for each diocesan synod to decide, and the Standing Committee cannot issue a direction on the point. But it is desirable that deanery synods should be consulted in view of the importance of the subject at the parochial level, and that they should be asked to vote by Houses on the same motion -*without amendment and as a single motion* - as has been prescribed for the diocesan synods. Discussion at parish level should also be arranged.

REPORTING ARRANGEMENTS

11. To enable the Standing Committee to report to the General Synod in time for the February Group of Sessions 1992, diocesan synods are asked to complete their consideration of the matter now referred and to notify the Secretary-General of their views by 30 November 1991. A report form will be sent to each Diocesan Synod Secretary under reference DC(90)8. Additional copies of the report form may be obtained on application to the General Synod office.

12. Diocesan Synod Secretaries are also asked, if possible, to supply the results of any voting in deanery synods; these figures are desired simply as background information.

DISCUSSION MATERIAL

13. The Standing Committee suggest that diocesan synod members should be given copies of this Memorandum (and the appended draft legislation) and that their attention should be specifically drawn to the existence of the House of Bishops Report (GS 829) and of the Digest (GS Misc 337).

On behalf of the Committee
W D PATTINSON
Secretary-General

Church House SW1
April 1990

Draft Priests (Ordination of Women) Measure

ARRANGEMENT OF CLAUSES

PART I
POWER TO LEGISLATE BY CANON

PART II
DISCHARGE OF FUNCTIONS

PART III
GENERAL

Draft
of a Measure
Proposed to be passed by
The General Synod of the Church of England

A.D. 1990
To make provision for the ordination of women as priests, and for connected purposes.

PART I
POWER TO LEGISLATE BY CANON

Provision for ordination of women as priests

1. (1) It shall be lawful for the General Synod to make provision by Canon for enabling a woman to be ordained to the office of priest if she otherwise satisfies the requirements of Canon Law as to the persons who may be ordained as priests.

(2) Nothing in this Measure shall make it lawful for a woman to be consecrated to the office of bishop.

PART II
DISCHARGE OF FUNCTIONS

Bishops

2. (1) A bishop of a diocese in office at the relevant date may make any one or more of the following declarations—

    (a) that a woman is not to be ordained within the diocese to the office of priest; or

    (b) that a woman is not to be instituted or licensed to the office of incumbent or priest-in-charge of a benefice, or of team vicar for a benefice, within the diocese; or

    (c) that a woman is not to be given a licence or permission to officiate as a priest within the diocese.

(2) A declaration by a bishop under subsection (1) above shall be contained in a written notice signed by him.

(3) A bishop who has made a declaration under subsection (1) above may by written notice signed by him withdraw the declaration.

(4) A copy of any notice given under subsection (2) or (3) above shall be sent to the following—

(a) Her Majesty;

(b) the Duke of Cornwall;

(c) the Lord Chancellor;

(d) the archbishop of the province concerned;

(e) the secretary of the diocesan synod of the diocese concerned;

(f) the registrar of the province concerned;

(g) the registrar of the diocese concerned;

(h) the designated officer for the diocese concerned, within the meaning of section 7(5) of the Patronage (Benefices) Measure 1986.

1986 No.3

(5) Where the bishop of a diocese who has made a declaration under subsection (1) above and not withdrawn it ceases to hold that office, the declaration shall continue to be in force until the expiry of a period of six months beginning with the date on which another person becomes the bishop of that diocese.

(6) Where a declaration by a bishop under this section is in force, a suffragan bishop discharging any functions of the bishop by virtue of an instrument under section 10 of the Dioceses Measure 1978 or a scheme under section 11 of that Measure shall act in accordance with the declaration.

1978 No.1

(7) A declaration under subsection (1)(c) above shall not prevent a woman from being allowed under any Canon of the Church of England to officiate as a priest in a church or chapel for a period of not more than seven days within three months without reference to the bishop or other Ordinary.

Parishes

3. (1) Subject to the following provisions of this section the parochial church council of a parish may pass either or both of the resolutions set out as Resolution A and Resolution B in Schedule 1 to this Measure.

(2) Subject to the following provisions of this section a parochial church council which has passed a resolution under subsection (1) above may by resolution rescind it, and the first-mentioned resolution shall continue in force until rescinded.

(3) A motion for a resolution in the form set out as Resolution A in Schedule 1 to this Measure shall not be considered by a parochial church council if the incumbent

or priest-in-charge of the benefice concerned, or any team vicar or assistant curate for that benefice, is a woman ordained to the office of priest.

(4) A resolution shall not be passed by a parochial church council under subsection (1) or (2) above unless—

(a) except where subsection (7) below applies, the secretary of the council has given to the members of the council at least four weeks' notice of the time and place of the meeting at which the motion proposing the resolution is to be considered; and

(b) the meeting is attended by at least one half of the members of the council entitled to attend.

(5) A copy of any resolution passed by a parochial church council under subsection (1) or (2) above shall be sent to the following—

(a) the bishop of the diocese concerned;

(b) the rural dean of the deanery concerned;

(c) the lay chairman of the deanery synod concerned;

(d) the registrar of the diocese concerned;

1986 No.3
(e) the designated officer for the diocese concerned, within the meaning of section 7(5) of the Patronage (Benefices) Measure 1986;

(f) the registered patron of the benefice concerned, within the meaning of section 39(1) of that Measure.

(6) Where a resolution under subsection (1) above is in force a person discharging any function in relation to the parish or benefice concerned shall act in accordance with the resolution.

1986 No.3
(7) The Patronage (Benefices) Measure 1986 shall have effect as if in section 11 (requirements as to meetings of parochial church council) there were inserted at the end of subsection (1) the following paragraph—

'(f) deciding whether to pass a resolution under section 3(1) or (2) of the Priests (Ordination of Women) Measure 19—.'

1952 c.xxxviii
(8) Subsections (1) to (6) above and Schedule 1 to this Measure shall apply in relation to a guild church designated and established under section 4 of the City of London (Guild Churches) Act 1952 as they apply in relation to a parish, but as if the reference to the parochial

8

church council of the parish was a reference to the guild church council of the guild church.

(9) In this section 'parish' means—

(a) an ecclesiastical parish; and

(b) a district which is constituted a conventional district for the cure of souls.

Cathedrals 4. (1) The administrative body of a cathedral church other than a parish church cathedral may pass either or both of the resolutions set out as Resolution A and Resolution B in Schedule 2 to this Measure.

(2) An administrative body which has passed a resolution under subsection (1) above may by resolution rescind it, and the first mentioned resolution shall continue in force until rescinded.

(3) A motion for a resolution under subsection (1) above in respect of a cathedral church shall not be considered by an administrative body if the dean or any of the residentiary canons of the cathedral church is a woman ordained to the office of priest.

(4) A copy of any resolution passed under subsections (1) or (2) above shall be sent to the following—

(a) Her Majesty;

(b) the bishop of the diocese concerned;

(c) the secretary of the diocesan synod of the diocese concerned;

(d) the registrar of the diocese concerned.

(5) Where a resolution under subsection (1) above is in force in respect of a cathedral church a person discharging any function in relation to the conduct of services in the cathedral church or in relation to the appointment of the dean shall act in accordance with the resolution.

(6) In this section 'administrative body', 'cathedral church' and 'residentiary canon' have the same meanings **1963 No.2** as in the Cathedral Measure 1963.

Ecclesiastical offences 5. It shall be an offence against the laws ecclesiastical, for which proceedings may be taken under the Ecclesiastical **1963 No.1** Jurisdiction Measure 1963—

(a) for any suffragan bishop to act in contravention of a declaration under section 2(1) above; or

9

(b) for any bishop, priest or deacon to act in contravention of a resolution under section 3(1) above or to permit any act in contravention of such a resolution to be committed in any church or any building licensed for public worship according to the rites and ceremonies of the Church of England; or

(c) for any bishop, priest or deacon to act in contravention of a resolution under section 4(1) above or to permit any act in contravention of such a resolution to be committed in any cathedral church.

Discriminatory discharge of certain functions
6. Without prejudice to section 19 of the Sex Discrimination Act 1975, nothing in Part II of that Act shall render unlawful sex discrimination against a woman in respect of—

(a) her ordination to the office of priest in the Church of England;

(b) the giving to her of a licence or permission to serve or officiate as such a priest;

(c) her appointment as dean, incumbent, priest-in-charge, team vicar or assistant curate.

Benefices in the patronage of the Crown etc.
7. (1) Sections 2 and 3 above shall apply in relation to a Crown benefice and to a benefice the patronage or a share of the patronage of which is vested in the Lord Chancellor as they apply in relation to any other benefice.

(2) The provisions of section 4 shall apply in respect of the appointment of any dean by Her Majesty.

1986 No.3
(3) In this section 'Crown benefice' has the same meaning as in the Patronage (Benefices) Measure 1986.

8. In this Part—

Interpretation of Part II
'benefice' includes—

(a) the office of incumbent of a parish church cathedral but does not include any other office in a cathedral church; and

(b) the office of priest-in-charge of a district which is constituted a conventional district for the cure of souls;

'relevant Canon' means the Canon enabling a woman to be ordained to the office of priest;

'relevant date' means the date on which the relevant Canon is promulged.

PART III

GENERAL

General interpretation

9. In any Canon, order, rule or regulation relating to priests, words importing the masculine gender include the feminine, unless the contrary intention appears.

Minor and consequential amendments

10. The enactments specified in Schedule 3 to this Measure shall have effect subject to the amendments specified in that Schedule, being minor amendments or amendments consequential on the provisions of this Measure.

Amendment etc. of Measure or Canon

11. A motion for the final approval of a Measure or Canon of the Church of England which amends or repeals any provision of this Measure or of any Canon promulged under section 1 above shall not be deemed to be carried unless it receives the assent of a majority in each House of the General Synod of not less than two-thirds of those present and voting.

Short title, commencement and extent

12. (1) This Measure may be cited as the Priests (Ordination of Women) Measure 19—.

(2) This Measure shall come into force on such day as the Archbishops of Canterbury and York may jointly appoint, but they shall not appoint a day for the purpose of this subsection unless a Measure of the General Synod making provision as to the relief of hardship incurred by persons resigning from ecclesiastical service by reason of opposition to the promulgation of a Canon under section 1 above has been enacted.

(3) This Measure shall entend to the whole of the provinces of Canterbury and York except the Channel Islands and the Isle of Man:

Provided that, if an Act of Tynwald so provides, this Measure shall extend to the Isle of Man subject to such modifications, if any, as may be specified in such Act of Tynwald.

Schedules

Section 3(1)

Schedule 1
Forms of Parish Resolution

RESOLUTION A

That this parochial church council would not accept a woman as the minister who presides at or celebrates the Holy Communion or pronounces the Absolution in the parish.

RESOLUTION B

That this parochial church council would not accept a woman as the incumbent or priest-in-charge of the benefice or as a team vicar for the benefice.

Section 4(1)

Schedule 2
Forms of Dean and Chapter Cathedral Resolution

RESOLUTION A

That the administrative body would not accept a woman as the minister who presides at or celebrates the Holy Communion or pronounces the Absolution in the cathedral church at any service other than [a service] held on the direction of the bishop of the diocese.

RESOLUTION B

That the administrative body would not accept a woman as the dean of this cathedral church.

Schedule 3

Minor and Consequential Amendments

Pluralities Act 1838

1. In section 36 of the Pluralities Act 1838—

   (a) for the word 'he' there shall be substituted the words 'such spiritual person';

   (b) after 'widow' there shall be inserted the words 'or widower'.

2. In section 43 of that Act for the word 'wife' in both places where it appears there shall be substituted the word 'spouse'.

Synodical Government Measure 1969

3. In Schedule 3 to the Synodical Government Measure 1969 (Church Representation Rules)—

   (a) in rule 16(3) there shall be inserted at the end the words 'or section 3 of the Priests (Ordination of Women) Measure 19—';

   (b) in rule 17—

   (i) in paragraph (1)(c) after '1983' there shall be inserted the words 'and its functions under section 3 of the Priests (Ordination of Women) Measure 19—';

   (ii) in paragraph (2) after 'Part I' there shall be inserted the words 'and its functions under section 3 of the Priests (Ordination of Women) Measure 19—';

   (c) in rule 17A—

   (i) in paragraph (1)(c) there shall be inserted at the end the words 'and its functions under section 3 of the Priests (Ordination of Women) Measure 19—, as may be so specified';

   (ii) in paragraph (2) after 'Part I' there shall be inserted the words 'and its functions under section 3 of the Priests (Ordination of Women) Measure 19—';

   (d) in rule 17B—

   (i) in paragraph (1)(c) after '1986' there shall be inserted the words 'and section 3 of the Priests (Ordination of Women) Measure 19—';

(ii) in paragraph (3) after '1986' there shall be inserted the words 'and section 3 of the Priests (Ordination of Women) Measure 19—'.

1978 No.1

Dioceses Measure 1978

4. In section 10(1) of the Dioceses Measure 1978 there shall be inserted at the end the words ', except functions under section 2 of the Priests (Ordination of Women) Measure 19—'.

5. In section 11(2) of that Measure there shall be inserted at the end the words ', except functions under section 2 of the Priests (Ordination of Women) Measure 19—'.

1983 No.1

Pastoral Measure 1983

6. In section 20(8) of the Pastoral Measure 1983 there shall be inserted at the end the words 'Provided that a woman who is a vicar in a team ministry shall not by virtue of this subsection have authority to preside at or celebrate the Holy Communion or pronounce the Absolution in a parish to which a resolution in the form set out as Resolution A in Schedule 1 to the Priests (Ordination of Women) Measure 19— applies'.

7. In section 21(1) of that Measure there shall be inserted at the end the words 'Provided that a woman who is the incumbent of a benefice shall not by virtue of paragraph (a) above have authority to preside at or celebrate the Holy Communion or to pronounce the Absolution in a parish to which a resolution under section 3(1) of the Priests (Ordination of Women) Measure 19— applies'.

8. In Schedule 4 to that Measure in paragraph 13(1)(c) and (3) for the word 'widow' whenever it appears there shall be substituted the words 'surviving spouse'.

1983 No.2

Church of England (Miscellaneous Provisions) Measure 1983

9. In section 8(1) of the Church of England (Miscellaneous Provisions) Measure 1983 there shall be inserted at the end the words 'and functions under section 2 of the Priests (Ordination of Women) Measure 19—'.

14

10. In section 11(2)(a) of the Patronage (Benefices) Measure 1986 for the word 'wife' there shall be substituted the word 'spouse'.

11. In section 12(4) of that Measure for the word 'wife' there shall be substituted the word 'spouse'.

12. In section 13(5) of that Measure at the end there shall be inserted the words 'Provided that this subsection shall not apply in respect of—

(a) a parish in a diocese to which a declaration under section 2(1)(b) of the Priests (Ordination of Women) Measure 19 applies; or

(b) a benefice comprising a parish to which a resolution under section 3(1) of that Measure applies,

where the refusal is made solely on grounds of gender'.

13. In section 35(7) of that Measure after the words 'traditions of the parish' there shall be inserted the words '(including the terms of any resolution under section 3(1) of the Priests (Ordination of Women) Measure 19—) affecting the benefice in question)'.

Draft Canon C 4B: Of Women Priests

1.   A woman may be ordained to the office of priest if she otherwise satisfies the requirements of Canon C 4 as to the persons who may be ordained as priests.

2.   In the forms of service contained in the Book of Common Prayer or in the Ordinal words importing the masculine gender in relation to the priesthood shall be construed as including the feminine, except where the context otherwise requires.

Draft Amending Canon No. 13

1.   In Canon C 2 (Of the Consecration of Bishops), there shall be added at the end the following paragraph—

'5. Nothing in this Canon shall make it lawful for a woman to be consecrated to the office of bishop.'

2.   In Canon C 3 (Of the Ordination of Priests and Deacons) paragraph 9 shall be omitted.

3.   In Canon C 8 (Of Ministers Exercising their Ministry), in paragraph 2(a) at the end there shall be inserted—

'but nothing in this sub-paragraph authorises
(i) a minister or sequestrator in a parish to which a resolution in the form set out as Resolution A in Schedule 1 to the Priests (Ordination of Women) Measure 19— applies, or
(ii) a dean or provost or the canons residentiary of a cathedral church to which a resolution in the form set out as Resolution A in Schedule 2 to the said Measure applies
to allow an act in contravention of that resolution to be committed.'

4.   In Canon C 10 (Of Admission and Institution), after paragraph 2 there shall be inserted the following paragraph—

'2A.   No bishop shall admit or institute a priest who is a woman to a benefice if a resolution under section 4(1) of the Priests (Ordination of Women) Measure 19— is in force in the parish concerned or, in the case of a benefice which comprises two or more parishes, in any of the parishes concerned.'

5. In Canon C 11 (Of Induction), in paragraph 3 for the words from the beginning to 'shall' there shall be substituted the words 'The archdeacon may'.

Draft Ordination of Women
(Financial Provisions) Measure

ARRANGEMENT OF CLAUSES

Draft
of a Measure
Proposed to be passed by
The General Synod of the Church of England

A.D. 1990

To make provision as to the relief of hardship incurred by persons resigning from ecclesiastical service by reason of opposition to the ordination of women as priests, and for connected purposes.

Entitlement to residential and financial benefit

1. (1) Subject to the provisions of this Measure, every person to whom this section applies shall be entitled, on application, to—

(a) participate, in accordance with section 2 below, in any church housing scheme; and

(b) receive from the Board financial benefit consisting of—

(i) a resettlement grant in accordance with section 3 below; and

(ii) periodical payments in accordance with section 4 below.

(2) This section applies to every clerk in Holy Orders, deaconess or licensed lay worker who—

(a) was in whole-time stipendiary ecclesiastical service (being service which is pensionable service for the purposes of the pensions regulations) within the Province of Canterbury (including the Diocese in Europe) or the Province of York at the relevant date or at any time during the period of six months immediately preceding that date;

(b) at the relevant date has performed a period of such ecclesiastical service of not less than five years or a succession of periods of such ecclesiastical service (whether with or without intervals) amounting in the aggregate to not less than five years;

(c) within the period commencing six months immediately before the relevant date and ending ten years immediately after that date has ceased to be in such ecclesiastical service consequent on his resigning therefrom;

(d) within the period of ten years immediately after the relevant date has made a declaration in the form set out in the Schedule to this Measure stating that he would not have resigned but for his opposition to the promulgation of the relevant Canon;

(e) has not attained the retiring age;

(f) is not in receipt of a pension under the pensions regulations.

Housing
1961 No.3

2. Section 26 of the Clergy Pensions Measure 1961 (powers of Board as to provision of residences) and any church housing scheme shall have effect for the purposes of this Measure as if—

(a) any reference in that section or scheme to a retired clerk in Holy Orders included a reference to a clerk in Holy Orders to whom section 1 above applies; and

(b) any reference in that section or scheme to a retired church worker included a reference to a deaconess or licensed lay worker to whom section 1 above applies.

Resettlement
grants

3. (1) A resettlement grant under section 1(1)(b) above shall be a single payment of an amount equal to three-tenths of the national minimum stipend or such greater amount as the Board may, with the concurrence of the Commissioners, determine.

(2) Such a grant shall not be paid unless the Board is satisfied that the applicant was, immediately before the material time, residing in accommodation made available to him in order to enable him to undertake the service from which he has resigned.

Periodical
payments

4. (1) Subject to subsection (2) below, periodical payments under section 1(1)(b) above shall be paid monthly to the applicant during a period expiring at the end of—

(a) such number of months immediately following the material time as results from adding together—

(i) one month for each year or part of a year during which the applicant has served in whole-time stipendiary ecclesiastical service; and

(ii) one month for each year or part of a year which has passed before the material time since the applicant attained the age of forty years; or

(b) thirty-six months immediately following the material time, whichever is the greater:

Provided that where an applicant has at the material time attained the age of fifty years the payments shall continue until, in the case of a man, he attains the age of sixty years or, in the case of a woman, she attains the age of fifty-five years, if the payments would otherwise cease before he or she attains that age.

(2) Such payments shall cease to be payable in respect of any person—

(a) when he attains the retiring age; or

(b) if he receives a pension under the pensions regulations before attaining that age, on the date on which the pension is first paid; or

(c) if he re-enters whole-time stipendiary ecclesiastical service as defined in section 1(2)(a) above.

(3) Subject to section 6 below, each monthly payment shall be of an amount equal to one-twelfth of the following—

(a) in the first period of twelve months, the national minimum stipend for the year in which the payment falls to be made;

(b) in the second period of twelve months, three-quarters of the national minimum stipend;

(c) thereafter, two-thirds of the national minimum stipend.

1972 No.5 (4) Regulations approved by the General Synod under section 6 of the Clergy Pensions (Amendment) Measure 1972 may make such amendments to subsection (1) above as the Synod considers necessary or expedient in consequence of any regulations made under subsection (1)(a) of that section.

Discretionary payments 5. (1) Subject to subsection (2) below, the Board may, on application being made to it by any person, provide such financial benefit to him by way of periodical payments, grant or loan or otherwise as it thinks fit.

(2) In the case of an applicant to whom section 1 above does not apply, the Board shall not make any payment under subsection(1) above unless it is satisfied that—

21

(a) within the period of ten years immediately after the relevant date, the applicant or any person on whom the applicant is (or was immediately before that person's death) dependent—

(i) has ceased to hold an office or employment or to be a member of a religious community consequent on his resigning therefrom; and

(ii) has made a declaration in the form set out in the Schedule to this Measure stating that he would not have resigned but for his opposition to the promulgation of the relevant Canon; and

(b) in consequence the applicant has suffered or will suffer financial hardship.

(3) For the purpose of determining whether any financial benefit should be provided under this section and, if so, the amount and form of the benefit the Board shall have regard to—

(a) the age and other personal circumstances of the applicant;

(b) any special need of the applicant in respect of housing;

(c) any special need of the applicant in respect of training for suitable employment;

(d) the extent to which the applicant provides or might reasonably be expected to provide financial support for any person dependent on him; and

(e) all other relevant circumstances of the applicant's case.

Reduction etc. of periodical payments on account of other employment

6. (1) Subject to subsection (2) below, if any person who is applying for or receiving periodical payments under section 1(1)(b) or 5(1) above accepts any office or employment, the Board may refuse the application or, as the case may be, may suspend the periodical payments or reduce the amount thereof so as to take account of the emoluments of or other benefits which arise from the office or employment.

(2) The Board shall not exercise any of its powers under subsection (1) above if the total annual amount of the emoluments in question and the periodical payments (if any) would in consequence be less than the national minimum stipend.

(3) It shall be the duty of every person who applies for or receives periodical payments under section 1(1)(b) or 5(1) above to disclose to the Board any office or employment which has been accepted by him and the terms thereof; and if he fails to do so and it appears to the Board that in consequence it has made periodical payments which otherwise it would not have made or periodical payments in excess of those it would otherwise have made, it may, without prejudice to its powers under subsection (1) above, direct the repayment of the amount of the payments or excess or such part thereof as it thinks just, and that amount shall be recoverable as a debt due to the Board.

Declarations and applications

7. (1) A declaration made for the purpose of section 1(2)(d) or 5(2)(a)(ii) above shall be signed and dated by the person making it in the presence of another person who shall also sign it; and a copy of it shall be sent to the bishop of the diocese concerned.

(2) An application for any benefit under this Measure shall be made in such manner as the Board may determine; and where a person is incapacitated from making such an application himself the Board may authorise some other person to make it on his behalf.

Finance and administration

8. (1) The Board shall administer the system of benefits established by this Measure, and the Commissioners shall pay to the Board out of their general fund such sums as are required by the Board for the payments to be made by it under this Measure.

(2) The Board shall carry out its functions under this Measure in consultation with the Commissioners and in accordance with such directions of a general character as the Commissioners may give; and where the Commissioners give any directions under this subsection they shall as soon as practicable cause a report thereon to be laid before the General Synod.

(3) Directions given by the Commissioners under subsection (2) above may include directions which appear to them to be requisite or expedient for securing a due balance between the liabilities likely to be imposed on their general fund by virtue of sections 2 and 5 of this Measure and the resources of that fund available for meeting those liabilities.

Provisions as to pensions

9. (1) Where a person has received periodical payments under section 1(1)(b) above, the period during which they are paid shall be treated as pensionable service for the purposes of the pensions regulations.

(2) Nothing in this Measure affects the entitlement of any person to receive a pension under the pensions regulations where he retires before attaining the retiring age.

Appeals

10. (1) An applicant for any benefit under this Measure who is aggrieved by a determination of the Board in carrying out its functions under this Measure may appeal against the determination to a tribunal constituted in accordance with subsection (4) below.

(2) Subject to subsection (3) below, on any such appeal the tribunal may affirm the Board's determination or make any other determination which could have been made by the Board; and if the Board's determination is not affirmed it shall give effect to the tribunal's determination.

(3) In respect of any determination made by the Board under section 5 above the tribunal shall not vary the Board's determination unless it is satisfied that the Board—

(a) has exercised its discretion on a basis on which no reasonable determination should have been made; or

(b) has failed to take into account some material matter, or has taken into account some irrelevant matter, where in either case in acting properly the determination of the Board would or might have been significantly different:

Provided that this subsection shall not apply where the tribunal considers that, in all the circumstances of the case, not to vary the Board's determination would or might result in an injustice to the applicant which would or might cause significant financial hardship.

(4) The tribunal shall consist of five persons nominated by the chairman of the House of Bishops, the chairman of the House of Clergy and the chairman of the House of Laity acting jointly from a panel of twelve members of the General Synod selected by the Standing Committee.

(5) The Standing Committee may make rules regulating the procedure and practice on or in connection with proceedings on an appeal under this section, including in particular the time within which an appeal must be lodged.

(6) Any rules made under subsection (5) above shall be laid before the General Synod and shall not come into force until approved by the General Synod, whether with or without amendment.

(7) Where the Standing Committee determines that the rules do not need to be debated by the General Synod then, unless—

(a) notice is given by a member of the General Synod in accordance with its Standing Orders that he wishes the rules to be debated,

(b) notice is so given by any such member that he wishes to move an amendment to the rules and at least twenty-five other members of the General Synod indicate when the amendment is called that they wish the amendment to be moved,

the rules shall for the purposes of subsection (6) above be deemed to have been approved by the General Synod without amendment.

1946 c.36

(8) The Statutory Instruments Act 1946 shall apply to any rules approved by the General Synod under subsection (6) above as if they were statutory instruments and were made when so approved, and as if this Measure were an Act providing that any such rules should be subject to annulment in pursuance of a resolution of either House of Parliament.

Interpretation

11.   (1) In this Measure—

'Board' means the Church of England Pensions Board;

'church housing scheme' means any scheme operated for the time being by the Board under section 26 of the 1961 Measure for the purpose of providing residences to retired clergy and church workers;

'clerk in Holy Orders' means any bishop, priest or deacon of the Church of England;

'Commissioners' means the Church Commissioners;

'licensed lay worker' means a person who has been admitted by a bishop as a lay worker of the Church of

25

England and who has been authorised by a bishop by licence to serve as such a worker;

'material time' in relation to a person who resigns from stipendiary ecclesiastical service is the time when he ceases to be in such service;

'national minimum stipend', in relation to any year, means the national minimum stipend recommended for the stipends of clergymen of incumbent status for that year in the Annual Report of the Commissioners as the Central Stipends Authority;

'pensions regulations' means regulations for the time being in force under section 6 of the Clergy Pensions (Amendment) Measure 1972;

'relevant Canon' means the Canon of the Church of England enabling a woman to be ordained to the office of priest;

'relevant date' means the date on which the relevant Canon is promulged;

'Standing Committee' means the Standing Cmmittee of the General Synod.

(2) In this Measure the following expressions have the same meaning as in the pensions regulations—

'pensionable service';

'qualifying period of pensionable service';

'retiring age';

'stipendiary ecclesiastical service'.

Amendment etc. of Measure
12. A motion for the final approval of a Measure which amends or repeals any provision of this Measure shall not be deemed to be carried unless it receives the assent of a majority in each House of the General Synod of not less than two-thirds of those present and voting.

Citation and extent
13. (1) This Measure may be cited as the Ordination of Women (Financial Provisions) Measure 19—.

(2) This Measure shall extend to the provinces of Canterbury and York, except the Channel Islands and the Isle of Man, but may be applied to the Channel Islands, as defined in the Channel Islands (Church Legislation) Measures 1931 and 1957, or either of them, in accordance with those Measures, and may be extended to the Isle of Man by or under Act of Tynwald.

Schedule

Form of Declaration

I [name of declarant] of [address of declarant], hereby declare that on [date of resignation] I resigned from [state nature of office, etc.] and that I would not have resigned but for my opposition to the promulgation of the Canon of the Church of England enabling a woman to be ordained to the office of priest.

[signature of declarant]

[date]

Signed and dated in the presence of

[name of witness] of [address of witness]

[signature of witness]

Explanatory Memorandum
on the Legislation

General

1. The legislative package consists of the *Priests (Ordination of Women) Measure,* draft *Canon C 4B,* draft *Amending Canon No.13* and the *Ordination of Women (Financial Provisions) Measure.* The first Measure deals with the principle of the ordination of women to the priesthood and also makes provisions as to decisions by bishops, cathedrals and parishes regarding the exercise of priestly functions by a woman in priest's orders. The second Measure deals with financial provision for those who resign from an office or employment because they cannot accept women priests in the Church of England.

2. The first Measure, dealing with the principle of women's ordination is, in part, an enabling Measure which permits the General Synod to promulge Canons providing for the ordination of women to the priesthood. This is dealt with in draft *Canon C 4B* and draft *Amending Canon No.13* referred to later in this Explanatory Memorandum.

Notes on Clauses

Draft Priests (Ordination of Women) Measure

Clause 1 makes it lawful for the General Synod to provide by Canon for enabling a woman to be ordained priest if she satisfies the normal requirements of Canon Law (as to age, for example) concerning those to be ordained priest.

Subsection (2) makes it clear that the legislation will not make it lawful for a woman to be consecrated to the office of bishop.

Part II of the Measure (clauses 2 to 8) contains a set of provisions designed to deal with the position of those bishops, cathedral chapters and parishes which continue, after the passage of the legislation, to be unwilling to accept the ministry of women in priest's orders.

Clause 2 gives a diocesan bishop in office when Canon C 4B is promulged the right to make all or some of a range of declarations. He may prohibit the ordination of women as priests in the diocese; he may prohibit a woman, wherever ordained, from being instituted or licensed as an incumbent, priest-in-charge or team vicar; he may prohibit a woman from being given a licence or permission to officiate in the diocese.

While one of these declarations is in force, it binds all in the diocese, including area and suffragan bishops *(sub-section (6))*; this latter provision preserves the collegiality of the bishops of a diocese. It does not, however, prevent an incumbent from exercising a power he already enjoys in respect of male priests of inviting a woman priest to officiate within his parish for a single period of not more than seven days in any 3 months *(sub-section (7))*; the power contained in Canon C 8 2(a) does not require the approval of the bishop.

Sub-section (3) provides for withdrawal by the bishop of such a declaration and *sub-section (4)* stipulates those who are to receive a copy of the declaration.

Sub-section (5) provides for a declaration to continue in force during the vacancy of a see and for six months after the bishop's successor takes office. The new bishop will not be able to make a declaration under Clause 2, and the six-month period allows clergy and parishes time to reflect upon the new situation in their diocese.

Clause 3 deals with parishes and *sub-section (1)* enables the parochial church council to pass either or both of the resolutions set out in *Schedule 1* to the Measure. The first resolution (Resolution A) prevents a woman priest exercising a priestly ministry in the parish by pronouncing the absolution or celebrating the Holy Communion; the second (Resolution B) prevents a woman priest from being appointed as incumbent or priest-in-charge or team vicar. They are given binding force by *sub-section (6)* which provides that persons discharging functions in relation to the parish or benefice must act in accordance with the resolution.

Sub-section (2) provides for such resolutions to be rescinded and *sub-section (3)* does not permit the parochial church council to consider passing Resolution A where a woman priest is serving in that parish as incumbent, priest-in-charge, team vicar or assistant curate.

Sub-section (4) lays down certain conditions which must be met before a parochial church council can pass either of the resolutions set out in Schedule 1. They are designed to ensure that a decision is reached after consideration by a well-attended meeting of the Council.

Sub-section (5) stipulates those who are to receive a copy of the resolution.

Sub-section (7) amends the *Patronage (Benefices) Measure 1986* so that, when a vacancy in the benefice occurs, the section 11 meeting of the parochial church council (when the parish statement is considered and the parish representatives are appointed) is also required to consider whether to pass a resolution concerning women priests or to rescind an existing resolution.

Sub-section (8) deals with guild churches in the city of London and *sub-section (9)* contains definitions. A conventional district is treated as a parish for the purposes of the Clause.

Clause 4 deals with cathedrals and *sub-section (1)* enables the administrative body of a dean and chapter cathedral (a parish church cathedral is covered by the provisions of clause 3) to pass either or both of the resolutions set out in *Schedule 2* to the Measure. The first resolution (Resolution A) prevents a woman priest exercising a priestly ministry in the cathedral except at a service held on the direction of the diocesan bishop; the second (Resolution B) prevents a woman priest from being appointed as dean of the cathedral.

Sub-section (2) provides for such resolutions to be rescinded and *sub-section (3)* does not permit the administrative body to consider passing such resolutions where a woman priest is serving as dean or as a residentiary canon of the cathedral.

Sub-section (4) stipulates those who are to receive a copy of the resolution and *sub-section (5)* provides that persons discharging functions in relation to the conduct of services in the Cathedral or the appointment of the dean must act in accordance with the resolution.

Sub-section (6) contains definitions.

Clause 5 makes the contravention of declarations and resolutions an ecclesiastical offence under the Ecclesiastical Jurisdiction Measure 1963.

Clause 6 ensures that compliance with declarations and resolutions under the Measure in relation to women is not unlawful under the provisions of the Sex Discrimination Act 1975.

Clause 7 contains the necessary special provisions which ensure that clauses 2 and 3 apply to a benefice in the patronage of the Crown or the Lord Chancellor and that clause 4 applies in respect of the appointment of a dean of a cathedral by Her Majesty.

Clause 8 contains definitions and *Clause 9* deals with interpretation. *Clause 10* deals with minor and consequential amendments of other enactments set out in *Schedule 3* to the Measure.

Clause 11 stipulates that no Measure or Canon which amends any provision of the Priests (Ordination of Women) Measure or the Canon promulged under clause 1 shall be deemed to be carried at final approval unless it receives a majority of not less than two-thirds of those present and voting in each House of the General Synod.

Clause 12 deals with the short title, commencement and extent of the Measure. Sub-section (2) ensures that it cannot come into force until the enactment of the Ordination of Women (Financial Provisions) Measure or a Measure to the like effect.

Draft Canon C 4B: Of Women Priests

Paragraph 1 gives authority for the ordination of a woman to the office of priest provided she satisfies the requirements of Canon C 4 as to those who may be ordained priest. The power enabling such a Canon to be promulged is contained in Clause 1 of the Priests (Ordination of Women) Measure.

Paragraph 2 provides for words importing the masculine gender when referring to the priesthood in the Book of Common Prayer and in the Ordinal also to include the feminine and for the substitution of the word 'she' where required.

Draft Amending Canon No.13

Paragraph 1 amends Canon C 2 to make it clear that a woman cannot be consecrated to the office of bishop.

Paragraph 2 amends Canon C 3 by revoking paragraph 9 which stipulates that it is unlawful for women to be ordained priest.

Paragraph 3 amends Canon C 8 in order to prevent a minister or sequestrator in a parish or the dean, provost or residentiary canon of a cathedral permitting a woman priest to officiate where a resolution has been passed refusing to accept the priestly ministry of a woman.

Paragraph 4 inserts in Canon C 10 a new ground on which a bishop may refuse to institute a priest to a benefice, namely that a parish in the vacant benefice has passed a resolution that it would not accept a woman in priest's orders as incumbent.

Paragraph 5 amends Canon C 11 by giving a general power to the archdeacon to authorise another clergyman to make induction on his behalf.

Ordination of Women (Financial Provisions) Measure

This draft Measure is designed to relieve hardship which might otherwise be incurred by those resigning from office or employment as a result of their opposition to the ordination of women as priests.

Clause 1 identifies a group of persons who are given the right to a standard set of entitlements specified in greater detail in *Clauses 2 to 4*. A person falling outside this primary group may be granted financial benefits under *Clause 5*.

Sub-section (2) defines those to whom the standard entitlements are to be granted. They are bishops, priests, deacons, deaconesses and licensed lay workers in whole-time stipendiary ecclesiastical service, who have completed five years of such service, and who declare (using the form in the *Schedule*) that they would not have resigned but for their opposition to the promulgation of Canon C 4B. Those who have already qualified for a pension are excluded.

Sub-section (1) lists the financial benefits to be made available. These are:

(a) participation in the scheme operated by the Pensions Board for the provision of housing to retired clergy (which may take the form of rented accommodation, or a loan secured by an equity-sharing mortgage) and to which *Clause 2* refers;

(b) for those living in a parsonage house or other official accommodation, a resettlement grant of an amount equivalent to 30 per cent of the national minimum stipend, as provided in *Clause 3*; and

(c) periodical payments under *Clause 4.*

Clause 4 provides for periodical payments to be paid at a level and for a period varying with the age and length of service of the applicant. In every case, periodical payments are available, for at least three years; for those resigning when over the age of fifty, entitlement continues until the age at which a pension becomes available under the clergy pensions legislation *(sub-sections (1) and (2))*. The maximum amount of the payment is fixed by *sub-section (3)*.

The level of periodical.payments is subject to *Clause 6.* This provides that the award of periodical payments may be refused, or the level reduced, on account of emoluments or other benefits received from some other office or employment. *Sub-section (2)* ensures that other emoluments or benefits are not taken into account if the effect would be to reduce the applicant's income (from the other office or employment and from periodical payments added together) to less than the national minimum stipend. The object is to give in all cases a 'safety-net', by guaranteeing a minimum level of income, but by withholding benefit when other employment is obtained and a satisfactory level of income arises from that source.

Sub-section (3) provides for disclosure of relevant information by the applicant.

Clause 5 enables the Pensions Board to award appropriate benefits at its discretion *either* to persons who do not fall within the standard group identified in Clause 1 but who meet the conditions of *sub-section (2) or* to persons within the standard group whose special circumstances require additional benefits over and above those provided under Clauses 2 to 4. Examples of the first use of the Board's powers would be the award of benefits similar to those in the standard package to certain holders of chaplaincy posts and certain lay employees of the Church who do not meet the conditions in Clause 1. Examples of the second use of the Board's power would be the award of additional grants for attendance at a course of re-training or to meet special expediture as a result of ill-health or the reasonable expectations of dependants.

Clause 7 deals with the administration of the Measure by the Church of England Pensions Board and *Clause 8* for the provision of the necessary funds by the Church Commissioners. *Clause 9* relates the provision of the Measure to other aspects of the clergy pensions legislation.

Clause 10 provides for a right of appeal against a decision of the Board to an appeal tribunal constituted as set out in sub-section (3). The remaining provisions of the Clause give an indication of the principles under which the tribunal will operate, and enable procedural rules to be made.

Clause 11 provides definitions.

Clause 12 makes provision as to amendment or repeal corresponding to Clause 11 of the Priests (Ordination of Women) Measure and *Clause 13* deals with the citation and extent of the Measure.

Draft Code of Practice

The House of Bishops has prepared this draft Code of Practice in the light of the terms of the draft Priests (Ordination of Women) Measure as revised by the General Synod in November 1989.

The draft Measure is now referred to Diocesan Synods for consideration. The House of Bishops believes it will be helpful for this draft Code of Practice to be available as the draft Measure is considered. It must be understood that the Code of Practice is not part of the legislation, and that it will be open to the House of Bishops to alter it or add to it in the light of experience and changing circumstances.

April 1990
On behalf of the House

+ROBERT CANTUAR:

Chairman

INTRODUCTION

1 (i) By the enactment of the Priests (Ordination of Women) Measure 19 , and its associated Canons, the Church of England has opened the order of priests to women. This entails that the order is a single whole and that women duly ordained priest share equally in the exercise of its ministry with their male counterparts and in consideration for suitable appointments.

(ii) The House recognises that there have been and will continue to be deeply held differences of conviction about the ordination of women to the priesthood and that some, bishops, clergy and laypeople, find it unacceptable. Christian charity and the exercise of true pastoral care require that careful provision be made to respect as far as possible their position while doing as little as possible to prejudice the full exercise of priestly ministry by women.

2. The Measure contains provisions designed to protect the position of individuals and parishes. It is important that those provisions are fully honoured. Some other matters are not easily or appropriately provided for in legislation, but are dealt with in this Code of Practice. This Code, therefore, complements but in no way qualifies or detracts from the legislation.

DECLARATIONS BY DIOCESAN BISHOPS

3 (i) It is a matter for each diocesan bishop in office at the date on which the Canon comes into force to decide whether or not to make any or all of the declarations referred to in Section 2 of the Measure.* Because of the effect of the declarations on his suffragans, and on the diocese as a whole, it will be appropriate for the bishop to consult with the other bishops in the diocese and with the Bishop's Council. It will, however, be recognised that the object of Section 2 is to protect the position of the diocesan and the decision is his alone.

(ii) The Measure provides that a suffragan bishop shall act in accordance with a declaration made by the diocesan bishop. Diocesan bishops who elect not to make any or all of the declarations provided will fully respect the views of suffragan, area and assistant bishops, as the case may be, in

---

*Section 2 of the draft Measure provides that a diocesan bishop in office at the relevant date may make one or more of the following declarations:

   (a) that a woman is not to be ordained within the diocese to the office of priest; or

   (b) that a woman is not to be instituted or licensed to the office of incumbent or priest-in-charge of a benefice, or of team vicar for a benefice, within the diocese; or

   (c) that a woman is not to be given a licence or permission to officiate as a priest within the diocese.

the diocese and will not expect or require any bishop to act against his conscience. The practices in some dioceses, particularly where there are Area Schemes, may have to be reviewed.

(iii) Each diocesan bishop will inform any area, suffragan or assistant bishop in the diocese, and the Bishop's Council, as to whether he has made any, or all, of the declarations provided in Section 2 of the Measure.

(iv) There may be diocesan bishops who, whilst not wishing themselves to ordain women to the priesthood, would not wish to inhibit such ordinations taking place in their dioceses. In such cases the diocesan bishop would not make the declaration provided in Section 2(1)(a) and would arrange for another bishop to ordain women to the priesthood in the diocese.

(v) Diocesan bishops will arrange, in preparation for the promulgation of the Canons, for the secretary of each PCC in their dioceses to be advised of the provisions made in section 3 of the Measure for parishes to consider Resolution A and/or B.

LAY WOMEN SEEKING ORDINATION TO THE PRIESTHOOD

4.   A lay woman wishing her vocation to the priesthood to be tested, and who lives in a diocese where the bishop has made a declaration that no woman is to be there ordained to the office of priest, may approach the bishop of a neighbouring diocese, normally that nearest her place of residence.

5.   The bishop to whom application is made, if prepared to pursue that application, shall inform the bishop of the candidate's own diocese that application has been made to him and invite the bishop to let him have any observations on the candidate. When the bishop to whom application is made has decided whether or not the candidate is to be sponsored for training, he shall inform the other bishop accordingly. If accepted, the candidate will be sponsored by the bishop to whom the application was made, who will accept the same financial responsibility for her training, as for that of all other candidates he sponsors.

6.   Where the application is in respect of Non-Stipendiary Ministry, a sponsoring bishop is required to undertake to find an appropriate placement. A neighbouring bishop approached by a woman candidate for NSM Ministry under this Code of Practice will have to consider the possibility of the candidate receiving a licence, which may depend upon her ability to move to his diocese.

WOMEN DEACONS SEEKING ORDINATION TO THE PRIESTHOOD

7.   A woman deacon wishing her vocation to the priesthood to be tested, and who lives in a diocese where the bishop has made a declaration that

no woman is there to be ordained to the office of priest, may approach the bishop of a neighbouring diocese, normally that nearest her place of residence. She shall first, however, inform her own bishop of her intention to make application to the neighbouring bishop for acceptance for the priesthood. If accepted the provisions of Canon C 5, paragraph 1, and of paragraphs 5 and 6 of this Code will apply.

ORDINATION SERVICES

8.   The conduct of ordination services, whether held in a cathedral or a parish church, is a matter for the ordaining bishop. He determines, after due consultation, where and when individuals are to be ordained and which priests should be present and take part in the laying on of hands.

9.   An individual ordinand cannot insist that other candidates should or should not be ordained at the same service. It would be inappropriate to exclude candidates of one gender from a particular ordination service, or to arrange a separate service for ordinands opposed to the ordination of women to the priesthood. However, in a number of dioceses ordinations to the priesthood commonly take place in the parish church of the parish in which a candidate is serving as deacon. Where a male deacon is serving in a parish which has passed Resolution A, this practice might be found especially helpful. It would be inappropriate to hold an ordination at which a woman deacon was to be ordained priest in the parish church of a parish which has passed Resolution A.

10.   Bishops commonly welcome the sharing in the laying on of hands by priests related to, or well-known to, individual candidates. Where an ordination takes place in a diocese where the bishop has made a declaration reflecting his continuing opposition to the ordination of women or in a parish where Resolution A is in force, the ordaining bishop would not invite a woman priest to take part in this way.

EXERCISE OF PRIESTLY MINISTRY IN A PARISH

11.   (i) Bishops will expect full and sensitive observance of the rights given to PCCs under the Measure and already enjoyed by incumbents under Canon Law. In particular, they will seek to ensure that rural deans and others arranging services in a parish will make no arrangements which would contravene a PCC resolution or override the wishes of the incumbent.

(ii) (a) In circumstances where the incumbent is ill or incapacitated the arrangements made for priestly ministry will be consonant with the incumbent's own past practice.

(b) During a vacancy in a benefice the practice which obtained prior to that vacancy will be continued, unless a resolution to the contrary is passed by the PCC under the provisions of section 3 of the Measure.

(iii) The House would regard it as an abuse of section 2 (7) of the Measure, and of Canon C 8, for an incumbent to use those powers to further a policy of a regular ministry of women priests in the parish(es) of his benefice.

OCCASIONAL OFFICES

12. The Measure enables a PCC to carry Resolution A declining to accept a woman as the minister who presides at or celebrates the Holy Communion in the parish. Where the Holy Communion is combined with a Marriage or Funeral Service, the House will expect incumbents to respect the wishes of those concerned as to the gender of the president, provided always that, if Resolution A has been carried, it must be observed.

EXTRA-PAROCHIAL MINISTRY

13. Before licensing a priest to a college, hospital or other institution under the Extra-Parochial Ministry Measure 1967, a bishop consults with the appropriate authorities of the institution. These consultations will cover the question of the acceptability of a woman priest where such an appointment is contemplated.

APPOINTMENTS AND MINISTRY IN MULTI-PARISH
BENEFICES, TEAM MINISTRIES, ETC

14. The body which makes the decision to pass Resolution A or B is the Parochial Church Council of a parish (or of a conventional district). A parish may, however, either be part of a larger unit comprising a single benefice, or contain within itself several churches, perhaps of differing traditions, which may or may not have formal District Church Councils. In these situations, and in some related cases such as Group Ministries, especial sensitivity will be required in making appointments.

15. The legislation provides that where a benefice comprises more than one parish, the passing of Resolution B by any one PCC prevents the appointment of a woman as incumbent of the benefice. This position must be respected by all concerned, but each PCC within such a benefice should recognise the effect and implications which carrying Resolution B will have for the benefice as a whole.

16. Resolution A applies only to an individual parish, and not to other parishes in the same benefice. Its existence will, however, limit the scope of the ministry of any woman priest serving within the benefice. The fact that one of the parishes had carried Resolution A would need to be carefully weighed before a woman priest was appointed.

17. Similar considerations apply in the case in which a parish contains churches of different traditions. Where a District Church Council exists it

may express a view on the matters covered by Resolutions A and B (though that expression of view would have no formal legal effect); where there is no District Church Council, the bishop may ask the incumbent and churchwardens to ascertain the balance of opinion within the congregation. It would be inappropriate to seek to appoint a woman as incumbent of a parish which contained a church whose congregation found her ministry unacceptable. The same would be true of the appointment of a woman team vicar or assistant curate whose area of responsibility would include that church; in other cases, where there were to be limitations on the area in which she was to exercise her ministry, an appointment of a woman to serve in the parish could still be appropriate.

DIOCESAN, ARCHDEACONRY AND DEANERY SERVICES

18.   Even where a resolution under section 4(1) of the Measure is not in force for the cathedral, bishops will seek themselves, and will encourage others, to be sensitive in making arrangements for diocesan, archdeaconry and deanery services in circumstances where women priests serve in the area but there are also significant numbers who find the exercise of priestly functions by a woman unacceptable. Where this latter position is known to be predominant it would be inappropriate for a woman priest to exercise those priestly functions; in other cases, the identity of the officiant should be made known in advance. If such practice is adopted, it should be followed whether the officiant at a particular service is female or male. Subject to that, when the clergy of an area, or the holders of particular offices such as that of rural dean or canon, are invited to robe, the invitation will apply in all cases without discrimination as to gender.

CARE OF THOSE WHO RESIGN FROM OFFICE

19.   The House affirms that its members will continue to be concerned for the pastoral care of, and the practical provision for, those clergy who make the declaration provided in the Schedule to the Ordination of Women (Financial Provisions) Measure. The House hopes that any deacon or priest who may be considering making that declaration, or who has concluded, in conscience, that he or she must do so, will continue to be in touch with the diocesan bishop of the diocese in which he chooses to reside.